W9-BFQ-451

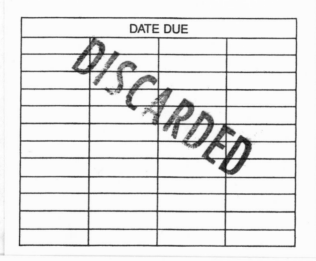

ANIMALS

POEMS BY

ALICE MATTISON

Library of Congress Catalogue Card Number 79-54884
ISBN 0-914086-29-4
Printed in the United States of America

Cover by Kathy White
Typeset by Jeffrey Schwartz
Paste-up by Ronna Johnson

I'd like to thank my mother, Rose Eisenberg; The Children's Co-op Daycare of New Haven; Susan Bingham; and especially my husband, Edward Mattison, for help, day after day, that gave me the time and the heart to write.

For permission to reprint some of these poems, thanks to the following publications: *Aspect, Green House, The Massachusetts Review, The New American Review, The Paris Review, Ploughshares, Red Fox Review, U.S. 1 Worksheets,* and *Women/Poems.*

The prose passage in "Timber Line Group" is from a placard entitled "Timber Line Group" in the Peabody Museum, Yale University, New Haven, Conn. The quoted material in "Secret Animals" is from *Pregnancy and Birth* by Alan Guttmacher, Viking Press, New York, 1962.

The publication of this book was assisted by a grant from the Massachusetts Council for the Arts and Humanities.

Alice James Books are published by
Alice James Poetry Cooperative, Inc.

ALICE JAMES BOOKS
138 Mt. Auburn Street
Cambridge, Massachusetts 02138

CONTENTS

I   Secret Animals

II   Other People

I Secret Animals

Secret Animals

By coincidence, the
summer of this pregnancy
is the time when the scientists choose,
once and for all, to find
the Loch Ness monster.
I read this morning they are using sonar,
a useful tool, the obstetrician tells me, for
gauging maturity
by determining the size of the head: "So
there won't be any surprises."
Nights, in the heat, I think about
"Rosa and Josepha, Bohemian twins born
in 1878," who "were
united at the base of the spine and had
a common rectum and vagina, though separate uteri."
Guttmacher says that as far as he knows, "They are the
only female pygopagi
to bear a child.
It is stated that the two had one
husband. At the age of thirty-two,
Rosa gave birth to a normal son, after
a very short labor. Josepha
did not experience
the pains of labor, and
both women were equally able

to nurse the infant. They died
a few hours apart in Chicago during
the influenza
epidemic
of 1918."

     The scientists grumble
in the Scottish summer morning,
eating the storybook food, the kippers and sausages.
Clumsy in their sweaters, their necks itching,
they go to bend over their instruments.
They can't get warm.
What plays with them
simple as a puppy
has never, like Josepha, for example,
lain in an accommodating posture, quietly,
to let the pregnancy of the sister
who is always behind
pass without sensation through
what isn't quite
her own vagina, but is
the vagina she has; what the
scientists are looking for
wouldn't say,
"I am a monster."

Husband

This headache
musters in my skull
slowly growing dense enough
to screen your face, but
your arms are sprouting like vines
dropping in coils on the rug
overgrowing the hidden backs of chairs
while, from the dusky tangle of arms
an occasional hand flashes.

Your legs jam the doorways
as rigid as fallen trees.

I remember speech with one source, but
your voice booms through the whole place
throwing echoes between my eardrums
throbbing through the air in my nose.

I know about lovers
whose kisses are collisions—
for us, there's an overlapping:
your smell is my climate
there is no new flavor

and look at your sperm
let loose all over the house
pursuing me like a swarm of gnats
stabbing my helpless unshelled eggs
so that sticky red spheres spring up from nowhere—

in every room,
children are emerging from jelly
fingers popping from shapelessness
children slipping loose from their membranes—
wherever I turn they knock against my cheeks.
I am a hollow tube
thrust into a bed of children
with children bubbling out at top and bottom,
crawling up my thighs, cascading
over my lips and down my shoulders,
prodding me inside and out with new feet.

I am going to bed
to press my own bones into the mattress.
I am going to be a fossil:
the place where I lie down
will be visible in rock.

Surgery

"Life cannot be managed
with so many emergencies.
Everything gets to you."
"You're right," I said.
"It's quite simple," he explained,
"a rearrangement of the interior
that eases the knots. . . ."

When my guts
billowed out over the table,
it took the nurse a long time
to pack them back in,
looping them on her arms,
trying to make sense of the tangle.
She held my insides down
while the doctor sewed me up.
Her elbow brushed across my face
as though she wasn't a stranger.
It smelled of an unfamiliar soap.

When I ate my jello, I felt it go down
at a new angle. They'd given me turns
that would have served their own tubes;
mine required a slightly more open curve.
It was like smelling the cooking
of someone else's mother.
There was a truce in my body,
but it wasn't mine.
It was like following advice.
If only my head would reach down.
I needed to lick it, to mark their work

with the rhythms of my tongue's muscle,
the perfect taste of my own saliva.

My intestines reweave themselves
into the old intricacy.
The traditional pattern
surfaces in sections,
is slowly completed.
The quiet goes
with the smell
of the nurse's hand lotion.

Life Kit

for Ben

pregnant
an eggplant
expanding like a popover
a pot boiling over
litter basket with a
swinging
top, piñata,
grab bag: secret inside,
little present, little fish worm
lying in his bubble
spinning his meconium, his
green shit

come right in
and let me weigh you, please, any
staining? one hundred
fifty-four, that's seven pounds
this month, please come this way,
the doctor will see you in a moment, just
leave me a sample and slip off
your panties
for me
okay?

in me
two urethras stretch toward one another
mine facing his; my channels
lead to the inhabited lake
where growth sets out

gardens of its own
I do not do
for you
I do for me, which is
his climate and geography

good morning, how are you?
good morning, how are you?
let's see how you feel
let's see how you feel
the head is still high
the head is still high
the heartbeat is steady
the heartbeat is steady
I really can't tell you
when you'll be ready

I think his toes
will poke out through
my belly button
sometimes I get nervous

you're gaining too much weight
you're gaining too much weight
I wonder what you ate
I wonder what you ate
aren't you going to hate
yourself so overweight?

No, I'm gorgeous
I am thin as string
like the young women
who walk around downtown
whose torsos are too narrow
for bladder or bowels, if you stick
your medical stick up their hole
it will get stuck—

get plenty of rest
get plenty of rest

I am gross as a garbage truck

Whoops, I just put on another pound

that will be all, take it easy
that will be all, take it easy

I'm a woman, I don't want
to take up space.
I want to stay home and dwindle.
Being is embarrassing; I cannot stand it—

their instruments probing my solidity
my bulk on their scales
my urine in their cups
oh dermatologists, dentists, ophthalmologists,
do what you like to me—
I admit to having eyes;
all function, so little flesh;
cool teeth; closed, dry skin—
but doctors of wet, warm places

that shake when they're pushed—
I don't like you.
I want to be broken glass
spearing someone's heel.

Wednesday? I'm sorry, Doctor
is out on Wednesday mornings
on Tuesdays, Doctor takes emergencies:
Thursday at ten: very well, good-bye

good-bye, good-bye, good-bye, good-bye
I have to go buy a bike horn
to mount on my belly
I have to go rent a billboard
and be drawn in the nude
I have to go buy a loudspeaker
and broadcast my noises

I walk out; I fill the doorway;
I'm terribly sorry; if you knew
what I'm really like—all I need
is a little path curving
around the wall when the door is opened
a crack; I'm a scurrier,
I'm an insect made of hair—

no, my body fills the doorway
my body treads the floor
my body is planted upon
an area taking up
about one sixth of the elevator
if somebody else tried to stand here
he couldn't do it: I am here already

I pilot myself
out into the street
where, again,
I do not vanish

I look at buildings, people,
buses and cars—
it occurs to me
that I am probably worth
this quantity of substance.
The self seeks
embodiment;
my body wields
self.
No, doctor,
I'm no bigger
than I ought to be;
the piece of air I borrow
is just my size.
I don't run around incorporating
matter I cannot live in.
This flesh
is the mouthpiece
for something true;
reality speaks
in, among other things, bellies;
I offer mine
it carries a present
it is a present.

Germchild

Her body lets go
onto the air,
that broth swimming with
slowly revolving treats—
with scalloped bacteria, varied
as colorful cogs and gears from an old invention,
with delicate spores, one crisp bite,
or bacilli, plump and fleshy, slipping down
like little clams, whose texture
stops at the luxurious
just short of the disgusting.
All her mouths open to the feast,
ready to sample the living populace
which will survive ingestion
to found its dynasties in the dark.
She's often called reckless, but she
trusts them, like the circus man
holding out his fingers
for the lions to lick.
Her ports of entry welcome immigrants:
ears, lined in orange like jewelry boxes,
nose, with its windblown reeds and viscous pools,
mouth, the great waterway to the interior,
yawning up tidal waves of quivering germs
like a whale sucking plankton, belly button,
a folded oyster, with room for one hard nugget,
vagina, with its plush, inviting walls and floor,
anus, dry and deep as an old well,
even the caves between the toes
gathering their soft stalagmites—

all these rejoice in the air,
spicy with inhabitants.
In peace, bacteria tumble and soar
in the playground of the amiable giant.
All the beasts let down their guard
and sleep like pets.

The Landlady's Complaint

These curly pated boys cooking semen like soup all day
Hoarding semen to dole out if any grateful girl
Curtseys by in a long skirt whispering "a boon, a boon"
These boys could make it in colors, they could sell it
They could preserve flies in hard bright beads of semen
They could pay the rent

what little they know of freedom
the bums, the semen squeezers

I once had a green scarf
Naked but for that feather
I waltzed in long loops
Down River Road: cars piled up
From here to Fulton, horns splattered
Around my ears; chunky jeeps, obese Pontiacs
Angled painfully around me
But I waltzed, those patrolmen pelting me with tickets
Could do nothing, shrugged and went home with all their
        flesh and metal

when I acted lighter than air
I was lighter than air
these boys can't do it

Now I'm the landlady and the land
Plowed and seeded, inhabited and milked
I know about children moving into me
Curling up in my tight space
I know about mouths taking milk from me
My arm supports a beam and my hand strokes the chimney
I'm the beam, I'm the chimney

these tired ones
trespassers
businessmen doing their business

Women are the land and the people

Nightmares in Northern California

"Take away the trees and this is just a suburb."—Robert

At night, from the road
you see woods, but a hundred yards in
beneath the pine trees
the mechanic is dreaming that the
overhead camshaft is upsidedown
he's been working on this car for weeks
he went to Sebastopol for two little screws
now he thinks it's perfect
he turns on the ignition
a healthy click, beginning of a nice hum
and then a WARP-BREAK-CRUNCH
car parts raining, raining
the fat girl in the T-shirt
is dreaming of her welfare worker
who comes pecking like a plier-beaked bird
they are the same age
in the dream they live together and drink coffee
Lynn seduces Sherry, which is easy
and it leads to no more kids
Edward dreams of a band of marauders
knifing him despite his good intentions
he turns and stabs back
it is like living in New York
Robert dreams of a captain with a big hat
Robert's the first mate, they tie up to go adventuring
what's a suburb? the place
where life slows down enough
to be recognized and picked apart

under the covers there is always the same tangle
bodies or souls, recalcitrant machines, dangerous people
you ride through and see all our trees
you think they give shape to our lives
you think somewhere there's a man surrounded by trees
whose gestures are simple because he is alone
by day he's a city all by himself
at night he's a suburb all by himself

Creatures

This morning a dying fish lay by the river
I didn't want to touch it
I pushed it into the water with a stick
it gulped air but lay on its side
the river kept tossing it at the sand
I poked it away
the current finally carried it off
with its live eye sideways.
Loading the washing machine, my hand bumped into
a gray and black mouse
dead like the one I found yesterday under my foot.
They are easy to crush and hard to scrape up.
Creatures keep dying, carelessly, next to me,
getting themselves on me:
crisp beetles,
dead birds with their stringy feet,
slugs oozing on the basement floor,
ready to burst if stepped on,
a moth dragging its own sticky belly,
a squirrel in the road, fur tossing in the wind,
groin turned up toward any scrutiny. They are
spring's irregulars, the young who don't
dry off and take flight,
their distracted relatives, caught
like shy celebrities trapped by the press,
flopped where anyone can look—
the carnival welter of hormones
was too much for their discretion.
The wildlife grows shameless in spring:
it's like putting out your hand in the dark
and feeling a penis.

Butt Gauges

are used to mount hinges on doors
alongside the melon ball scoop
hard-boiled egg slicer
jodhpurs, corn-skewers
tuning fork, grapefruit knife
kaopectate
nut pick
they wait for their single summons
practising saying "coming!"

as a matter of fact, consider
grinding stones
washboards
napkin rings
who may never again be called

those with particular adaptations
Latin teachers stuck in Alaska
learn not to hold their breath
or keep an eye on every browser

haven't you ever slipped between lives?
full of energy, competent,
you had one challenge—
to wear the uncut day
hanging so loosely around your shoulders
gracefully till bedtime

small objects, if they are kept clean
take pride all day
having done nothing to speak of

a human being
even without a future
is worth hanging onto

but to make a life of that shelf
chatting about the shelving paper
the view when the cupboard door is opened—
how does one keep from thinking about
hard stuff meeting one's good sharp blade
the cold shock of use?

The Guidebook

Fernand Lamaze
was a French obstetrician who, admiring
the Russian method of delivering babies,
brought it to his country. It has become popular
in many American cities.
It involves the conditioning of the mother;
you take a course, learning to
relax your muscles, and to breathe
in certain rhythms; these techniques
actually do alleviate pain; your husband, or
another coach, is present
throughout your labor and delivery.

The birth is messy. Nurses
keep changing pads under your bottom.
Later, you get a bill for them.

The main deprivations are:
in the first year, sleep
in the second year, daytime sex
in the third year, privacy
in the fourth year, conversation.

The greatest gains are these:
you can touch and fondle it all over
without embarrassment.
At certain stages,
it does something funny very often.
Taking care of it
justifies you,

if that is necessary.
Although some of the things it likes are boring,
others are fun.

After a while
you stop thinking it will suddenly die.

The shit *is*
disgusting, but not always. Small breastfed babies
have a mild, yellow, non-smelly shit.
Older children
often have a firm shit, which you can just
drop from the diaper
into the toilet, and, eventually,
they do learn to
take care of it all themselves.
Diarrhea
is hell.

The Other One

One morning I wake up and my name is in the paper.
I have gotten married.
I have married a stunt man from the movies.
Then I remember a remark, at that time incomprehensible,
by a salesclerk noting the name on my charge card:
"Oh, like in 'The Men and the Boys.'"

It turns out there is a newly famous sexpot with my name.
Suddenly our name is everywhere.
She is the latest thing.

This is especially hard for me.
I am an extremely private person.
She models one piece bathing suits in a national magazine—
        not one piece all over;
some are just bottoms, with a narrow arm of fabric that
wanders diagonally across the chest.
Others are only tops.

She does a billboard
in which she sprawls on her back
with her legs spread; she is
upside down.
The caption says, "I'd lie to get a Geddy." It's a soft drink.

I have about ten conversations with friends about how I feel.
I tell each of them, "At first it was just embarrassing.
Now I'm starting to feel responsible for her."
One of them thinks in some way I may have brought it on myself.

Once I am taken for her
by a nine-year-old boy at the opening of his father's
        one-man show of acrylics.
I sign the guest book.
Ten minutes later: "Hey, Dad, guess who came?"

She divorces the stunt man and marries a singer.
She gets a terrible review in her latest movie, which is not fair;
she did the best she could.

Not only is she photographed nude for a famous girlie magazine,
but she allows the photographer to lie on the floor
with his camera below her crotch.
The picture, her head looming in the distance, is startling.

Finally she divorces the singer. Now she's alone
with her fifteen-month-old daughter, Samantha.
I can no longer do anything dignified.

Even telling you this—you aren't interested.
Do you realize that this woman has my exact name, even the
        odd spelling?
No I cannot change my name at this late date.

Here I've been trying to confide this problem to you.
You act as though it's an ordinary situation.
You act as though I made it up.
You're thinking you'd rather be listening to *her.*
You think she'd have so much to say to you.
Well that's where you're wrong.
She'd like me much better.
She'd find me fascinating.

II Other People

Spells

In the next apartment
someone played a jazz piano;
hearing it, I knew I'd
lie in bed all day,
waste my life:

that spoiled, city music,
energy with the eyes closed—

it stays in the mind, mocking, like
the shouts of aimless laughter that
used to come into my head
when I was a child. I
never thought that, in the
dramatic sense, I "heard voices"; but
I couldn't make the laughing stop.
My gentle interior self,
always crooning repetitious talk
to get me home from school—
how could it turn against me?
—an elephant, rearing, falling on its
mad season.

Now I know who laughed, or
who knew how to
make themselves heard.
Even now, I hear them making a joke.

She makes a joke and squeezes
me up against that man—whose side
of the family?—who cannot understand
my name, though I am saying it
over and over; it begins to sound like nonsense, but he demands
whether I can't say my own name. . . .

It was a tremendous snowstorm.
The schools were closed on my birthday.
Aunt Ruth gave a party for Stuart
who had enlisted in the Air Force.
I'm sure that Stuart cheated Neil
a few years later, when Neil worked for him.
I never was close
to either of them. My cousins are
distant by two mothers.
"The esteemed aunts," I said.
"The steamed aunts," said Neil,
"like steamed clams."

They are the party, beckoning, moist, the
plumpness at the center, while
dim, eccentric uncles and
cousins known
for their
birthdays, efface themselves
like napkins or
collapsible serving tables.

It is a family of aunts.
When I am five, I am a little afraid
of calling the wrong one mommy; there are so many,
they are so much alike—
leaning into the birthday parties.

Even now, they're in their circle, keeping
color, thickness, tone:

Neil was right, but
he wasted money, and he
treated Aunt Esther terribly that summer;
and Marilyn never even called—
she could have picked up the telephone.

3

The piano played family music, crying about
passengers on the same line
being jostled
against one's bones

happy birthday, by this time
shouldn't the candle grace your skin?
we see you cannot touch the flame
we make a note

37

happy birthday, by next year
we suppose you're going to fly in through the window
we're making
a special adjustment to the drapes, believe us
we'll be looking

what did you say had made you tired? on
the phone, your voice could be Ellen's
happy birthday, remember when Marilyn
couldn't find the newspaper?
when Edgar couldn't find the cat?

you aren't singing on pitch
you never could

The sound of family
clings, like
icing in the mouth, hanging on,
ruining my supper.
Surely that crony
is privileged by blood, the one who's
making herself at home in my head—
laughing, laughing, singing happy birthday.

One to One

The men worked in the yard
dragging sacks of leaves
talking of what wasn't there.
They had lubricated joints
they had their own difficulties.
Indoors, Harriet and I cooked:
her left arm came up
between mine, stretching over
my left arm to stir the pot
while I peeled long strips
from vegetables, my arms
around her left arm, her right hand
handing my left hand potatoes, eggplants,
squashes, apples, and beets.
We turned to each other, to rest,
our feet crouched behind our ears,
sucking our belly buttons, surrounded
by our bodies, mugged by our flesh,
looking through screens, packed for shipping,
our limbs outlines, wings of a frozen chicken.
"Tell me about yourself," we said.
Skeins of yarn, we sought a starting place.
It was useless to try getting out—
knotted, corked, our bodies still
hold our past, loom everywhere. "Two grandmothers,"
I said, "Aunt Sarah, Aunt Phyllis,
Aunt Harriet, Aunt Helen, Aunt Clare,
Aunt Florence, Aunt Evelyn, Aunt Ina,
Aunt Barbie, a mother, a sister."
She said, "Two sisters, a mother,
No grandmother, Aunt Sylvia, Aunt Frances."

Shaking the Past

Turn the key and bolt the door,
Sweet is death forevermore. . . .
All is now secure and fast;
Not the gods can shake the past.
                              —Emerson

"I think you'll find
it isn't so much fear as prudence," he said,
once more counseling fear: sure enough, all week
I watched myself going downstairs
to check, again, the door I knew I'd bolted.

There were forms to fill out, lines, a fee.
Relation to self: father.
Periods of excision: you could pick any four
particular events, or a
blind package of ten—
but you'd never know what they were;
a machine makes a random selection.
What to choose?
No need to cut from the first years: a
maroon rug, a radiator bubbling. . . .
I could remove
his warning that I might
get polio from eating a
plum while
lying on my back: but surely he didn't
say that; he said that
touching my genitals
would bring on an infection—
"I can't remember the worst things,"
I told the clerk.

40

"Better take the package."
In the end, I did, rather than stand there all day.
Reason for petition: the door
won't stay closed; what happened
barges into the present,
still happening.
The court appearance
took just a few minutes, and
excision was accomplished:
ten unidentified
incidents between us
had not
occurred. They said I'd just have to
bring him in to be registered.
I drove home, perhaps
a little less nervously than usual.
The next day I went and got him.
"What do you want, oblivion, like
a teen-ager taking dope? What
are you, afraid of life?"
I didn't need to answer
and I began to feel
fond; he was a dear, funny old
guy; wasn't that just
what he *would* say? It wasn't far—
an official room—
"This is moronic." I left him there
with the other fathers,
he with his eccentric look,
his full head of hair, his slimness—
but when I turned back at the doorway,
with so little gone
he looked like all the others.

The Day in New York

for Bob

The upper level ladies' room at
Grand Central is still closed
I eat some lunch at Chock full o' Nuts
and go to spend my
birthday money, to buy the dress that
sums me up, but
of course it isn't there;
the one I try on is terrible.
I wear my feet out in the stores
watching the
confident teenage girls
laugh at the one I almost choose
and when I give up, it's so late
the museum is almost ready to close
god what a fool
but then I meet you
for dinner. Not even
bothering with wine, we eat, talk
walk back to Grand Central.

You tell me about your aunt.
I met her
once, when your brother was still fat.
You aren't trying
to change yourself. I talk about my
sister, whom you knew
before the hospital, or Los Angeles.
I don't need anything from you

but we're
each other's
stroke of luck; what we share
is nothing much
not drink,
or sex.

To a Well-Known Poet

I'd never heard of you until one day
when we were still trying to sell our
house in Forestville. We were browsing in a
bookstore in Berkeley, and I
saw one of your books, and liked it, so I
bought it. We drove over to the park to meet Mickey,
and took him home so he could wash for dinner.
He rode in the front seat, because he's tall;
I was in the back. He picked up your book
and read out loud from it a little. At his house
he went upstairs alone. I got into
the front seat (he said he'd use his own car),
and looked around for the book, but it wasn't there.
I thought Mickey had taken it by mistake,
but he came out without it, and
without his shoes; they were
in the trunk of his car, but he'd forgotten
his keys, locking himself out
of both the car and the apartment. He didn't
remember taking the book. We went to dinner
with Mickey in his socks. His friend Laurie,
who met us at the restaurant, drove him home,
after we ate, to look for the janitor.
A week later, we sold the house, and left
for the east coast. We didn't see
Mickey for two years. By that time
he'd moved, and his new house
had burnt down to the ground
with everything in it.

"Three Ways to Boil Brown Rice"

—Package Directions, **River** *Brand Brown Rice*

Three ways to boil the rice, but
only two ways to
turn a key in a lock:
even the time we tried
to walk around the Modesto Reservoir,
we kept saying we could always go back—
but not after the cows,
because I was afraid of them.

Still, with the loss of alternative
comes the need
for rescue. It was dark and cold by then;
we'd gone around
still another
finger of water that stretched
into the muddy fields
—my socks were wadded up under my feet—
and what was now in our way
was clearly the river that
feeds the reservoir—how could we
not have assumed—?
                    but then,
the campfire on the opposite shore,
the kids with their beer.

We shouted.
Amused, they flagged down the sheriff,
who poured their beer into the water

(you have to be twenty-one in California)
but sent for a rowboat to fetch us.

Of course, one of the kids
turned up as my student
the following fall.

Letting oneself be saved, one gets, again,
that surprise: there actually are
other people—
                and yet I
hold on to choices, afraid of
the spot where
bumping and sloshing in the dark, it's
somebody else's boat coming.

Three Novembers

Danny in the Hospital

after
visiting Danny in the hospital
I walk to Chapel Street.
The crazy teenagers stand in front of the Mall, in the cold.
White girls flirt with the black boys.
One girl is fat and has strange speech.
The black girls
call out something I don't catch.

he has gotten so deft with his tubes and poles;
in his tropical gown, he
shepherds them all to the bathroom

She cannot get the boy to look at her.
Her kneesocks only come so far, and the
pleated skirt is as short as the nuns will allow.
She moves one cold leg
over the other, pretending that
the flesh that's hidden by her knee
doesn't exist: or if the fatness of one leg
were two legs—

suddenly, I can't imagine
Danny ever cold
as though even his past
has been taken into another context
where bodies swell and glow for the surgeon
lit like a stage

47

2
Danny's Year

Winter again; you're alive,
periodically sick from the therapy,
but now it's over.
After the last test, the news is good.
We get together, the two couples, and open
a second bottle of wine with dinner.
Size of a grapefruit, and yet they are gone:
you caught the best kind of cancer.
The advances, these ten years, have been amazing. You feel
idle and swollen, drugged and punched. Deb
is angrier than ever, it makes no sense,
but she can't help it. What do they give you in exchange?
Life
you had when you came in, and without all these
after alls, this
balance, this
preposterous maturity.

3
Danny in my Kitchen

What is it—two years
since you got sick. I imagined you dead, but not
limping; no one mentioned
side effects.
When you stand up, it's clear your legs are bad.
Thanks, you say, you've already eaten; no,
not even coffee. At least you want
to borrow our socket wrench.
You're on your way
to shop for a new couch: having suffered
guarantees you nothing; the store
could be closed. . . it's as likely as if
you had no claims on luck. What can I wish you?
An attractive fabric, sturdy construction, a good price?
a couch where you may sit
for hours, unmoving, and not
have your foot fall asleep?
I know of no comfort that lasts, and
nothing I can give or lend
but the wrench, nothing
big.

Raspberries in New Hampshire

I am mentioning, long distance, my vacation.
She remembers raspberries.
"There were so many, it was ridiculous.
In the city, they were something like eighty-nine cents
a half-pint.
We cleaned out the bottom of the hill
and by the time we came down again
new ones had gotten ripe.
I must have eaten about ten dollars' worth.
Going back to Amy's, it was tiring,
with all the pails; I wasn't looking around
until we came to an open place—you know, rolling hills, fields,
—I said to Amy,
This kind of technicolor scene with the
green filter is so unreal—"

Her doctor now allows her
one egg, yogurt, cottage cheese, an apple,
chicken once a day, protein supplement, lots of tea.
Before this it was brown rice, lettuce, grapefruit, lemon,
        chicken, and
limited tea.
The diet before that
was steak, lettuce, tunafish, bacon and eggs.

I always forget how tall she is.
She's going to hug the whole house.

Why does she seem unlike anyone else?
Is it because she's my sister, trapped in my mind, for example,
in the category "younger"
though she's older than most of my friends?
She does not bring the container of cottage cheese to the table, but

spoons some into a bowl.
She cannot be hurried.
She does not laugh at herself. "I am not"
she points out, in my head,
"funny." Perhaps she does laugh at herself.
In that sweeping gesture, almost dangerous—
I see restraint; the shoulder looks awkward; the elbow?
So much I'm afraid to say to her:
"You could squeeze the lemon on the chicken—"

"No, I could *not*"—the sarcasm coiling out of the phone—
"ask Marilyn to come early. I know she'd
hate to do that sort of thing.
There are only two possibilities—
either I'll do the one or the other."
"But surely she'd realize— Surely there are other choices—"
"No, she wouldn't. There aren't any other choices."

I introduce her to a friend, who'll
comment later on her
energy, her beauty.
I know when she's nervous; she says her o's oddly.
These days she doesn't eat raspberries
but she's the one
who moves to L.A. and buys herself a condominium
or goes to visit our talky relatives,
making them cook what she eats.

The Facts

The washing machine was in the basement.
When the baby was small,
she used to carry him down
on top of the clothes.
Now he was too big,
so the laundry never got done
but if she found a sitter,
she could get some time
and even do the laundry:
she could write letters, read—
work on those poems. The sitter,
Jean, had light steps. The poems
took up all the time.
The drier warmed the basement.
She'd carry down the dirty clothes,
a cup of coffee, the typing paper.

They moved away.

                    From the new place,
which didn't have a basement,
she could bike to the library,
but there was no coffee; typing
wasn't allowed. The sitter, Ann,
after a week, got a better job.
There was a daycare co-op.
The mother wrote two poems.
A new child awakened
kicked inside her belly
broke her rhythm; she napped,

wrote, napped again.
The baby was born.
He slept, and woke up gradually,
giving her time to wind down.
There were lots of poems.
He began to wake all at once;
the poems had no ends.

She left him with a sitter, Kathy,
and typed in an unused room
in a church. The janitor,
each time, brought in
an empty wastebasket.
Once, he picked up some mud
that had fallen from her boots.
The next time, when she came,
a man's coat was folded
on her table. For half an hour
she thought of accounts of herself,
her typewriter, her thermos of coffee
to give to the man, if he came back.
He didn't come, but the time after that
she carried the typewriter up
to the attic of Susan's house.

No one came in.
At the window,
branches scratched:
spring came
the branches budded;
leaves
pawed at the window;

the attic was hot—
the poems made no sense.
Kathy, in any case,
went to White Plains.

The mother looked at her baby.
He laughed. She took both kids
to the daycare co-op.
She went home.
She had three hours.
She made coffee.

The Breadwinner

Man on train: Who is the breadwinner in your family?
Edna: We are all breadwinners.

"You've won the bread!"
I stride toward the platform,
cupping my hands over
the mouths of the cheering audience.
The announcer is concluding,
"and though she doesn't
park worth a damn, she does have a driver's license
and when she shops downtown, the store detectives
don't keep an eye on her. . . ."
but enough of that: I smile,
reaching across him to tear up
his notes, which I don't need any more:
I'm done with trying
to break into sufficiency, counting my efforts,
always detecting new strength.
I take my loaf, brimming with this
adequacy, this
ordinary
grace, laughing it off, posing reluctantly,
making light, talking with my mouth full.

The Grown-up

the year
I moved out of their house
I remember how things
were always about to explode: cars
parked outside my building
were ready to blow up, with fenders
clattering to the sidewalk right in front of me
—but I
did very
well; once, the bottom of the iron
was going to shoot through the air between my hands.
I could have done anything, that year—
bought cakes, skipped meals, but even in my new
privacy, I was nondescript.
One day a washing machine in the laundromat
groaned, and prepared to
split, like a big
eggshell, like
someone giving up—flinging hot water and clothes, and
at night, that year,
I'd lie in bed, mapping out how I'd be so quick
I'd grab my bathrobe, my notebook, my big brown pillow
and dive for the window, when, at last,
the furnace would let go.

The Crazy Baby

I have a nice baby but he is crazy.
On Monday he gets up from his nap
at two-thirty.
I need another half-hour, I was
just about to do something.
I will not see reason.

On Tuesday it's even earlier.
On Wednesday
he is dead, I drown him in the tub, like the woman in the paper.
I give him a bath.
I tell him, "I didn't drown you."

On Thursday he is still asleep at four.
I check again, but he is breathing.
There is nothing to do, I finished the book an hour ago.
I could clean something. I could masturbate.
Perhaps he is in a coma.
Now he is up.
We have no issues, he and I, but life,
death; not stabbing him with the pin,
I change his diaper; not being eaten,
I let him suck.
I tell him, "Oh you dodo, you
crazy baby."

The Bureau of Motor Vehicles

The state now requires
a photograph on your driver's license
which expires in the month of your birthday.
A notice comes in the mail. I go and stand on line,
prepared to surrender
my old license. In front of me in line
are more men than women, but there are several women,
among them someone I once knew a little.
She is about to be married.
"I'll be twenty-six next week," she says. My birthday
is next week too—oh,
of course. Renewing their licenses
I see many Puerto Ricans, few blacks.
Do blacks prefer not to renew their licenses
on Thursdays? Have they fewer birthdays in March?
Then I see
more blacks, as the line behind me
grows. A clerk accepts
what I've brought, she has me sit,
my name is called. I try not to smile, thinking how foolish
I'll look, smiling, some day, if a policeman asks.
A light flashes. I sit again. My name is called. I'm given
a small, solid, laminated card.
In the picture, I look as though
I am trying to keep my glasses from falling off
by stretching my nose—but everyone seems nervous, even those
short, square men in their shiny black jackets and sideburns,
          who are
unlike me, I am sure, who drive every day, who never are afraid
or in awe of the car which always will seem, to me,
gigantic, its obedience always surprising.
I put the new card in my wallet. I'm ready for
my birthday. I leave; we all leave,
all us Pisces.

Breastfeeding

It is like watching Yehudi Menuhin on television.
You see a round face,
mute, busy,
with the look in the eyes
people have when they're paying
close attention, but not
visual attention.
Next to the face, tipped up from the chin
and near enough to the mouth to make your
view seem intimate, what with the musician's
folded handkerchief (almost as if for dribble)
is something with a curved edge, about as big as
the face, soft in one instance, hard in the other; your breast, or
the violin. It is a crowded picture because
also, in the closeup, is the conductor's elbow, or
your own, which often gets in the way
(especially if you're lying down to nurse) and which looked,
on television, as though it might
bump into the violin, although, of course,
it must actually have been well in front.
Your arm is in back of your breast.
You don't feel the milk coming out,
nor see it;
what you see is someone else
drinking—thwarted music: played
elsewhere. When the milk,
however, starts to flow freely,
after the baby's been sucking for twenty seconds,
you feel, for a moment, as though your breasts
have been inflated, and you get that
sweet tension in your throat—as if there's something good
that you can't remember.

This Summer

I am very pregnant.
There is a spider in the bathroom.
Supper defrosts, slowly, on the counter.
One child chases the other;
the spider is still there.
How can you understand this? It
is so personal.
The child inside moves across my front
trying to straighten his knee.
At last, I take them all outside;
I steer my belly, my children
along the street:
we are so many ships.
We knock against the sidewalk.
We are so many stones.
Old women on stoops, shouting it's a boy, a girl
fall backwards away from us; the
dusty trees
tip backwards.
Only the heat gathers around us and sticks.
We roll home, three
wet balls of weather,
sloughing off our edges
trying to squeeze through the doorway.

Mary-Ellen

The person who works with pre-schoolers should have a lively
interest in the development of children, not to mention a flair
for practical thinking and organization.
    —R.C. Barton, *New Forms of Child Care,*
    New York, 1973, p. 82.

The morning gets warmer.
Puddles of sun
stretch across the yard. Still, it
seems to me,
Beth needs
the jacket. "No, Pumpkin."
"Why not?"
"It's really still cold."
This is not
the kind of thing I think about.

I don't have fantasies about children, except,
very occasionally,
of rocking an immaculate, motionless
baby, or of
hitting a child who doesn't resist, who
becomes docile.

I'm just not interested, on the whole,
in anything I can't
daydream about.
I'm not interested in law, for instance.
I'm not interested in institutions.
I really don't think I'm interested in children.

I cannot make Beth hurry, and I cannot make Maggie slow down;
yesterday we took them for a walk, and Beth
got slower and slower, poking elaborately at
parked cars; all I could do
was dance next to her in place, unable to wait.
Of course Maggie can't wait either,
and I can't make them different,
nor coax myself to shape
a pearl of growth
around this irritation.

As a child, I used to tell
stories to myself: "She
hurried down the street, her
blue skirt rustling
about her legs, the cold air stinging her cheeks. . ."
I rarely got past the setting,
but even there, I
reshaped
everything: my skirt
was long, and the cars were wagons, and
the place was country. I walked in a fairy tale, with no
race or religion, machines, government,
no institutions, divorce, or politics.
It was the
old days of the old days.

That patter comes easy, the private tongue
in which one stays at home
but the children are strangers; they speak
an impenetrable language.

Last week, I dreamed
I kicked Matthew—

and the mark
on his thigh
grew gray and purple, and more
and more like my shoe:
you could see the eyelets, and
the line of the laces; when his mother came,
she cradled him at my feet, silently,
looking from the picture to the real thing.

It was one more
dream about myself.

I want to be different:
to think without prompting about
suffering people, groups of people, anyone else.
The inside of my head
—intricate, absorbing—
just cannot be
the only good subject.

The old time is where
the self lives alone
and has never heard of history.
I want new fantasies.
I want my mind to outgrow
the language in which it's stuck:
like a two year old,
it can't risk
fooling around with its own safe laws;
my mind
squats over the sandbox,
hugging its toys.

Singing

He was so resistant that he walked
half a pace behind me, and stood still
when I waited for him to catch up.
Even so, we got through most of the shopping—
but when he asked me whether I'd
remembered the cheese, I got angry;
I minded his refusing to let me take charge
even while he was backing off himself.
"Look, if it bothers you, David," I said, "Don't stay."
"You don't understand. You think I'm being selfish.
What's left, anyway?"
"Not much. You go—just leave me the car."
"You don't understand."
"David, why don't you just go?"
"Well, if you're sure you want me to—"

So there I was, alone in the shopping center,
where the piped-in music always makes me feel
like a character in a musical, and then,
in fact, a crowd of shoppers began
to shuffle into a line, half of them
sticking out their right arms,
the other half their left.
Storekeepers skipped to the doors, with
clerks leaning jauntily out of doorways,
all moving as one
right on the beat
with no more
conference
than a wink and a gesture:

"Well times are bad, they're mighty bad
And prices are up, oh dear it's sad
And business is poor, and as I said
Times are bad—"

"Gotta bake that bread!"
(I didn't know
the man from the bakery could sing, or
that it was
made on the premises)
"Yes times are bad—gotta *buy* that bread!"

—a woman in a pantsuit.

But apparently this was all introductory,
because they grouped around *me*,
then drew back.
Everything got quiet. I was standing in front of a dress shop.
It was my cue.

"The mannikin in the window
Stares out into space
She doesn't smile, she doesn't frown—
If I were in her place,
'Alone' would be
Just right for me
But I'm not she—
I cry when *he*
Hurries from the place—"

Rot, I thought, and went on to buy the wine.
The clerk looked up expectantly.

            ". . . This party of mine—will it sparkle?
            Will awkwardness turn into play?"

            "Without any trouble, like soapsuds you'll bubble
            At the smell of our fine cabernet!"

            "Maybe gin, maybe rum—here's to liquor!—
            Have you anything special in Scotch?"

            "If you want your guests' speech to get thicker,
            Just pour, then some more, then you watch!"

            "And if someone should tickle my fancy
            Or my marriage should open a crack
            (If you see what I mean)—"
                    "This chianti—
            You'll be tickled to Thursday and back!"

Well, it was the end of the scene,
but when I drove up to the house,
the neighbors were all
hanging off their porches by one arm,
singing "Saturday," waving hoes and shovels.
Housewives came rushing down the
middle of the street, swinging their skirts,
grouping for a kind of square dance:

"—You gotta plant the seeds
—You gotta pull those weeds
Oh yes it's the end of the week
Just time for a kiss on the cheek—"

Boys of about twelve
were dancing in a circle with my grocery bags,
dropping them one by one on my porch.
It was quickly clouding up, though, and
as it grayed, they slowed, and finally
dispersed in an offhand way, and sauntered
casually but evenly out of the circle,
whistling, their hands in their pockets,
moving more and more slowly.
I looked to see
what was the big buildup.
It was David
standing still at the end of the block,
and the rain starting to fall.
I walked
to meet him, forgetting my pocketbook
and we began to sing

"Sweetheart—
We're going to—
Get a little wet together—
Sweetheart—
I thought you knew
You always get some stormy weather—"

Here, the rain came down in torrents,
we started dancing,
and all the neighbors

burst out, smiling, from their houses,
gathering around us, dancing, singing—

> "Well, friends, we're going to, me and you,
>   me and you—
> Get a little wet—don't get upset—together—
> But sweetheart—when your—man's with you—
>   gal's with you—
> Who cares—who cares—about any old weather?"

—and the music got faster and faster, and
then we were quiet
holding out our arms;
our hair
was plastered to our heads.
David and I shook hands perfunctorily
with most of the neighbors.
I could see he thought I was
overdoing it. I wished he were
friendlier.
They headed for their doorways.
Some had brought towels and were
rubbing down their hair and faces.
The rain had stopped; the music was gone.

Early Morning in Billings, Montana

It was gray; the air was just cool; the sky
hung above me like the inside of a skull.
It was easy to walk down that street.
Before I thought, I had entered
the brain of all the strangers
but it had relaxed, it was not like noon
with differences glaring in the sun.
I rarely enter the minds of others
but at dawn it seemed all right.
When a woman passed me,
not noticing me, not noticing that
she'd never seen me before,
I happened to glance at her mind;
she wasn't thinking in sentences—
squibs of color followed one another,
nearly blending. Blue for faded jeans,
the word "laundry," or the beginning of it,
pink which formed itself into a picture
of stained pink underpants, white
that broke up like soapsuds, gray
that was a street, and then I saw
it was the street she had just crossed
with a laundromat near the corner,
the flash of a man's big orange hands,
quickly erased from her mind.
Then she was gone. It was getting sunny.
I walked around till breakfast time,
went back to the motel, woke Ed up.
We ate at the Sambo's, much like the one
in Modesto, except for the position
of the booths and counters, which were
reversed, and drove out of that town.

Timber Line Group

We're walking from here
to where we thought we'd go.
The eyes look frontwards.
Other people
press against the glass
but cannot get to me.
And when I tell myself
that the different one has come
at the different hour—
when I turn to face you—
the message is
dismissed without question:
my eyes focus over your shoulder
and will not try anything new.

Here on this excursion,
here in the natural history museum
I have no idea what you'd like to look at.
When I try to know your mind
it is like picturing
a house I've never seen—
I get the basic shape wrong:
I imagine my own house.
You have nothing to say
but you aren't paying attention.
There's no chance of your seeing
what I happen to see.
I take you, anyway,
to the bighorn sheep.

"This scene illustrates the timber line zone as it occurs in northern latitudes around the world. Here, at midday in December, from an altitude of nine thousand feet, we look across a valley in the Ghost River region of Alberta, Canada. High altitudes, low temperatures, and steep slopes make this environment unfavorable for forest plants and many animals. Bighorn sheep, *Ovis canadensis*, are characteristic here. Living on rocky screes as in the foreground, wild sheep feed on grasses, herbs, and the leaves and twigs of stunted bushes, the only vegetation at this altitude. The old ram, possessor of fairly large horns, was in his eleventh year, and the young ram, fully mature, between three and four years old. Bighorn sheep normally live about seven years in the wild. These sheep were collected December 14, 1957 by James Simpson, an Alberta guide."

I never even see
men and women working around me
until they start to hammer.
They have opened one of the showcases.
They are carrying pheasants and quails away
being watchful of the feathers.
A young man, with exaggerated care, pries up
papier mâché bushes with a chisel.
The rocks are picked up and meticulously labelled.
When the showcase is empty, a man
lays some linoleum tiles that look familiar.
Where have I seen that pattern recently?
A woman in khaki pants
is carrying in our kitchen chairs.
A man is bringing our children,
one on each arm: he has given them lollipops.
The sitter is behind them, looking guilty.
A woman with a sheaf of papers
is speaking to you.
Another man supports my elbow,
helping me in:

71

the family is shown
at eight a.m. in south
central Connecticut
the father
is opening his mouth to take
a bite of toast the
mother
spoons cereal into the
baby's mouth the
older child
between three and four years of age
overturns his orange juice
this group was collected
on May 10, 1974

And that's how we came here.
I, so unlike the stereotype—
I, who tried so hard—
I'd knock a hoof on the glass
to know that it's really there
if I could just lean over.